Editor
Leasha Taggart

Editorial Manager
Karen J. Goldfluss, M.S. Ed.

Editor-in-Chief
Sharon Coan, M.S. Ed.

Cover Artist
Jessica Orlando

Art Director
Elayne Roberts

Art Coordinator
Denice Adorno

Product Manager
Phil Garcia

Imaging
James Edward Grace

Publisher
Mary D. Smith, M.S. Ed.

SO-BIT-112

How to Add & Subtract

Grade 3

Author

Mary Rosenberg

Teacher Created Resources, Inc.
6421 Industry Way
Westminster, CA 92683
www.teachercreated.com

ISBN-1-57690-944-1

©2000 Teacher Created Resources, Inc.
Reprinted, 2005
Made in U.S.A.

Table of Contents

A Note to Teachers and Parents

Welcome to the "How to" math series! You have chosen one of over two dozen books designed to give your children the information and practice they need to acquire important concepts in specific areas of math. The goal of "How to" math books is to give children an extra boost as they work toward mastery of the math skills established by the National Council of Teachers of Mathematics (NCTM) and outlined in grade-level scope and sequence guidelines. The NCTM standards encourage children to learn basic math concepts and skills and apply them to new situations and to real-world events. The children learn to justify their solutions through the use of pictures, numbers, words, graphs, and diagrams.

The design of this book is intended to allow it to be used by teachers or parents for a variety of purposes and needs. Each of the units contains one or more "How to" pages and two or more practice pages. The "How to" section of each unit precedes the practice pages and provides needed information such as concept or math rule review, important terms and formulas to remember, or step-by-step guidelines for using the practice pages. While most "How to" pages are written for direct use by the children, in some lower-grade level books these pages are presented as instructional pages or direct lessons to be used by a teacher or parent prior to introducing the practice pages. In this book, the "How to" page details the concepts that will be covered in the pages that follow, as well as how to teach the concept(s). Some of the "How to" pages also include "Learning Tips." The practice pages review and introduce new skills and provide opportunities for the children to apply the newly acquired skills. Each unit is sequential and builds upon the ideas covered in the previous unit(s).

About This Book

How to Add & Subtract: Grade 3 presents a comprehensive overview of addition and subtraction of numbers on a level appropriate to students in grade 3. The clear, simple, readable instruction pages for each unit make it easy to introduce and teach basic addition and subtraction to children with little or no background in the concepts.

The use of manipulatives as visualization is encouraged. In addition, if children have difficulty with a specific concept or unit within this book, review the material and allow them to redo troublesome pages. Since concept development is sequential, it is not advisable to skip much of the material in the book. It is preferable that the children find the work easy and gradually advance to the more difficult concepts at a comfortable pace.

The following skills are introduced in this book:

- adding and subtracting to 18
- adding 3-, 4-, and 5-digit numbers with and without regrouping
- reading and writing numbers with decimals to 2 places (tenths and hundredths)
- adding 3-, 4-, and 5-digit numbers with decimals
- place value to 6 places (ones, tens, hundreds, thousands, ten thousands, and hundred thousands)
- fractions
- writing fractions as decimals
- reading and using information (data) from a chart

- making conclusions based upon gathered information
- problem-solving skills and strategies
- estimation
- rounding numbers to the nearest ten, hundred, or thousand
- developing math-reasoning skills
- communication of math ideas through pictures, numbers words, charts, and tables
- number sense
- patterns
- using calculators
- using the Internet

The units in this book are designed to match the suggestions of the National Council of Teachers of Mathematics (NCTM). They strongly support the learning of addition, subtraction, and other processes in the context of problem solving and real-world applications. Use every opportunity to have students apply these new skills in classroom situations and at home. This will reinforce the value of the skill as well as the process. The activities in this book match the following NCTM standards:

Problem Solving

The children develop and apply strategies to solve problems, verify and interpret results, sort and classify objects, and solve word problems.

Communication

The children are able to communicate mathematical solutions through manipulatives, pictures, diagrams, numbers, and words. Children are able to relate everyday language to the language and symbols of math. Children have opportunities to read, write, discuss, and listen to math ideas.

Reasoning

Children make logical conclusions through interpreting graphs, patterns, and facts. The children are able to explain and justify their math solutions.

Connections

Children are able to apply math concepts and skills to other curricular areas and to the real world.

Estimation

Children explore estimation strategies and develop the skills to determine when it is appropriate to use an estimate and if an estimate is reasonable for the given situation.

Number Sense and Numeration

Children learn to count, label, and sort collections as well as learn the basic math operations of addition and subtraction.

Concepts of Whole Number Operations

Children develop an understanding for the operations (addition and subtraction) by modeling and discussing situations relating math language and the symbols of operations (+ and –) to the problem being discussed.

Whole-Number Computation

Children are able to model, explain, and develop competency in basic facts, mental computation, and estimation techniques.

Geometry and Spatial Sense

Children are able to describe, model, draw, and classify shapes and relate geometric ideas to number and measurement ideas.

Other Standards

Children use **measurement** (time, distance, weight, volume, area, etc.) and estimates of measurement in problem solving and in everyday situations. Children learn about **statistics** and **probability** as they collect and organize data into graphs, charts, and tables.

Children develop concepts of **fractions** through the use of pattern blocks. Children are able to recognize, describe, and extend a variety of **patterns** as well as represent and describe math relationships.

Learning Notes

In this unit children practice adding and subtracting to 18. They explore the concept of the Commutative Property and make math problems based upon information read from a paragraph.

Materials

- number line (0–20) or hundreds number chart
- counters (multilink cubes, buttons, chains, toothpicks, etc.)

Teaching the Lesson

Using the Commutative Property (page 7): Have the children show 10 + 5 using counters. Then have the children show 5 + 10 using counters. Ask the children what they noticed. (*Both 10 + 5 and 5 + 10 equal 15.*) Explain to the children that when adding numbers, the numbers can be added in different orders and the answer is the same. Have the children practice making different addition problems based on the Commutative Property before completing the work sheet.

Using Fact Families (page 8): Before doing the word problem on page 8, complete the following activtiy with the children.

Fact Family

A *fact family* is a set of math problems that use the same three numbers. For example, the numbers 1, 13, and 14 can be used to make two addition problems, 1 + 13 = 14 and 13 + 1 = 14, and two subtraction problems, 14 − 13 = 1 and 14 − 1 = 13.

Use these numbers to write fact families.

3	12	15		8	3	11
7	8	15		11	2	13
4	10	14		8	2	10

When adding 0 (zero) to an addend, the answer (sum) is always the same as the addend.
Example:

14	+	0	=	14
addend	+	addend	=	sum

Write the answer to each addition problem.

1. 0 + 18 = _____   3. 16 + 0 = _____   5. 14 + 0 = _____   7. 7 + 0 = _____

2. 10 + 0 = _____   4. 11 + 0 = _____   6. 3 + 0 = _____   8. 0 + 9 = _____

Write the missing addend.

9. _____ + 0 = 15   11. 0 + _____ = 11   13. 17 + _____ = 17   15. 13 + _____ = 13

10. 0 + _____ = 12   12. 10 + _____ = 10   14. 0 + _____ = 8   16. 6 + _____ = 6

When subtracting 0 (zero) from a number, the difference is always the same as that number.

Example:

14 − 0 = 14

14 is the difference for 14 − 0.

Write the answer to each subtraction problem.

17. 12 − 0 = _____   19. 17 − 0 = _____   21. 11 − 0 = _____   23. 16 − 0 = _____

18. 4 − 0 = _____   20. 9 − 0 = _____   22. 8 − 0 = _____   24. 15 − 0 = _____

Write the missing number.

25. 14 − 0 = _____   27. _____ − 0 = 10   29. 18 − _____ = 18   31. _____ − 0 = 6

26. 13 − _____ = 13   28. 7 − _____ = 7   30. _____ − 0 = 17   32. _____ − 0 = 5

Add or subtract? Write the missing + or − sign.

33. 9 _____ 5 = 4   36. 13 _____ 3 = 10   39. 11 _____ 6 = 17   42. 17 _____ 9 = 8

34. 12 _____ 3 = 15   37. 4 _____ 9 = 13   40. 10 _____ 0 = 10   43. 8 _____ 8 = 16

35. 7 _____ 5 = 12   38. 15 _____ 6 = 9   41. 8 _____ 8 = 16   44. 5 _____ 9 = 14

Numbers can be added together in any order without changing the answer. This is known as the **Commutative Property.**

For example, in the number sentences 6 + 8 = 14 and 8 + 6 = 14, the numbers 6 and 8 are added together in different ways, but the answer is still the same (14).

Write the answer to each addition problem.

1. 12	**2.** 6	**3.** 9	**4.** 8	**5.** 7	**6.** 11	**7.** 9	**8.** 5
+ 6	+12	+ 8	+ 9	+11	+ 7	+ 5	+ 9

9. 13	**10.** 1	**11.** 10	**12.** 5	**13.** 3	**14.** 15	**15.** 14	**16.** 0
+ 1	+13	+ 5	+10	+15	+ 3	+ 0	+14

Write the math problem for each of the word problems.

17. Janie has 7 pigs.

She buys 5 more pigs. **+**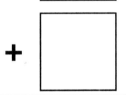

How many pigs does Janie have now?

18. Bill gathered 5 eggs.

Then he gathered 7 more eggs. **+**

How many eggs does Bill have now?

19. What did you notice about the two word problems?

_____

_____

20. Write two math problems using the numbers 5 and 8. Use the Commutative Property.

_____ + _____ = _____   _____ + _____ = _____

Write two addition problems and two subtraction problems for each Fact Family.

1.   3, 7, 10

_____ + _____ = _____

_____ + _____ = _____

_____ − _____ = _____

_____ − _____ = _____

2.   4, 9, 13

_____ + _____ = _____

_____ + _____ = _____

_____ − _____ = _____

_____ − _____ = _____

3.   2, 15, 17

_____ + _____ = _____

_____ + _____ = _____

_____ − _____ = _____

_____ − _____ = _____

4.   6, 11, 17

_____ + _____ = _____

_____ + _____ = _____

_____ − _____ = _____

_____ − _____ = _____

5.   1, 16, 17

_____ + _____ = _____

_____ + _____ = _____

_____ − _____ = _____

_____ − _____ = _____

6.   5, 13, 18

_____ + _____ = _____

_____ + _____ = _____

_____ − _____ = _____

_____ − _____ = _____

Write the missing + or − sign.

7. 3 _____ 4 _____ 2 = 5

8. 14 _____ 7 _____ 3 = 10

9. 6 _____ 5 _____ 0 = 11

10. 9 _____ 6 _____ 11 = 4

11. 18 _____ 13 _____ 1 = 6

12. 11 _____ 5 _____ 8 = 8

Read the paragraph below. Answer each question by writing the correct math problems.

> Farmer Jan has 6 sheep, 3 hens, and some horses. She has 16 animals in all.

13. How many horses does Farmer Jan have? _____

14. How many more sheep than hens does Farmer Jan have? _____

15. Does Farmer Jan have more horses or hens?_____

16. How many fewer sheep than horses does Farmer Jan have?_____

17. Which is more, sheep + hens **or** sheep + horses? _____

18. Which is less, sheep − hens **or** horses − sheep? _____

Learning Notes

Children learn and practice the vocabulary of math. They compare numbers using the symbols greater than (>) and less than (<) and use ordinal numbers to determine place or location.

Materials

- pictures from magazines or catalogs
- scissors
- pocket chart (optional)
- heavy paper
- glue
- heavy paper

Teaching the Lesson

Go over the math vocabulary with the children: addend, sum, minuend, difference, greater than, and less than. Ask the children if they know what the words mean. Use math problems to illustrate the meaning of each word.

For example, using the equation 3 + 9 = 12, ask: "Children, what are the two addends in this problem?" and "What is the sum of the two addends?"

Another example is 12 – 9 = 3. Ask: "Children, what is the difference?" and "What is the minuend?" Write 3 > 0; 4 > 0; 1 < 5. Ask the children if they notice a pattern. Ask: "What is the pattern?" and What does the pattern mean?" Tell the children that the < and > symbols mean less than and greater than. The large opening always points towards the larger number. Read the number sentences aloud, "3 is greater than 0; 4 is greater than 0; 1 is less than 5."

Do this several times with different math problems so that the children feel comfortable using the words.

Have the children cut pictures out of catalogs and magazines. Glue each picture on a peice of heavy paper. Place the pictures in a line on the chalkboard ledge, in a pocket chart, or on a table. Have the children pick up the picture that is third in line, first in line, last in line, 19th in line, etc. Explain that these words are ordinals. *Ordinals* tell the place or location of something.

Go over each work sheet with the children.

first

second

third

fourth

fifth

Ordinals

Math has a special vocabulary that is used to describe numbers and different math processes.

In addition, the two (or more) numbers being added together are called **addends**. The total of the two numbers is called the **sum**.

$$123 \quad + \quad 140 \quad = \quad 263$$

$$\text{addend} \; + \quad \text{addend} \quad = \quad \text{sum}$$

Write the answer to each addition problem. Use a green crayon to circle the addends. Use a blue crayon to circle the sums.

1. 123	**2.** 160	**3.** 407	**4.** 525	**5.** 222	**6.** 709
+ 300	+ 125	+ 312	+ 330	+ 333	+ 270

Read each word problem. Answer the questions.

Josephine collected 227 green rocks and 352 red rocks. Josephine has 579 rocks in all.

7. What are the two addends? _____ _____

8. What is the sum? _____

Diego has 419 fish stamps and 560 jelly fish stamps. Diego has 979 stamps in all.

9. What are the two addends? _____

10. What is the sum? _____

Read each word problem. Write the two addends and the sum.

11. Bill took 255 pictures on Monday and 400 on Tuesday. How many pictures did Bill take in all? _____

12. Sally collected 158 seashells today and 511 yesterday. How many seashells does Sally have now? _____

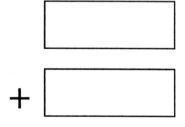

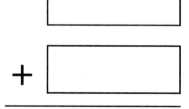

2 ▶ Practice • • • • • • • • Using Subtrahend, Minuend, and Difference

Math has a special vocabulary that is used to describe numbers and different math processes.

Subtraction is the process of removing one amount from a larger amount. The number that is being subtracted from is the **minuend**. The number being removed (or taken away) is called the **subtrahend**. The answer is called the **difference**.

$$567 \quad - \quad 231 \quad = \quad 334$$

$$minuend \; - \; subtrahend \; = \; difference$$

Look at the subtraction problems below. Use a red crayon to circle the difference.

1. 871	2. 985	3. 860	4. 358	5. 711	6. 651
– 550	– 674	– 260	– 117	– 400	– 330
321	311	600	241	311	321

Read each word problem. Answer the questions.

Reginald had 749 stickers. He gave 539 to his brother. Reginald now has 210 stickers left.

7. What is the minuend? _____

8. What is the difference? _____

9. What is the subtrahend? _____

Sophie planted 428 sunflower seeds. The crows ate 118 of the seeds. There are only 310 sunflower seeds left to grow.

10. What is the minuend? _____

11. What is the difference? _____

12. What is the subtrahend? _____

Read each word problem. Write the math problem and the difference.

13. Jerome saved 567 pennies. He spent 246 pennies at the toy store. How many pennies does Jerome have left?

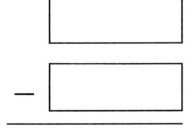

14. Cecilia had 821 buttons in her collection. She gave 301 buttons to her friend. How many buttons does Cecilia have left?

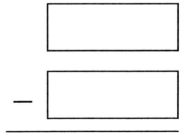

2 Practice • • • • • • • Using Greater Than, Less Than, and Ordinals

Math has a special vocabulary that is used to describe numbers and different math processes.

When comparing 2 sets of numbers, the > (greater than) symbol or the < (less than) symbol can be used. Below are examples of how to read these math sentences.

$$281 > 100$$

281 is greater than 100.

$$417 < 551$$

417 is less than 551.

Use the > or < symbols to compare the numbers below. Complete each sentence. The first one has already been done for you.

1.
376 (>) 259

___376___ is greater

than __259__ .

2.
923 ( ) 675

_____ is greater

than _____ .

3.
987 ( ) 255

_____ is greater

than _____ .

4.
550 ( ) 777

_____ is less

than _____ .

5.
800 ( ) 250

_____ is greater

than _____ .

6.
205 ( ) 353

_____ is less

than _____ .

7.
148 ( ) 579

_____ is less

than _____ .

8.
315 ( ) 188

_____ is greater

than _____ .

Ordinals are words that are used to describe location. For example: She is *fourth* in line. Fourth is the ordinal. Fourth tells where the girl is in line.

Answer the questions below.

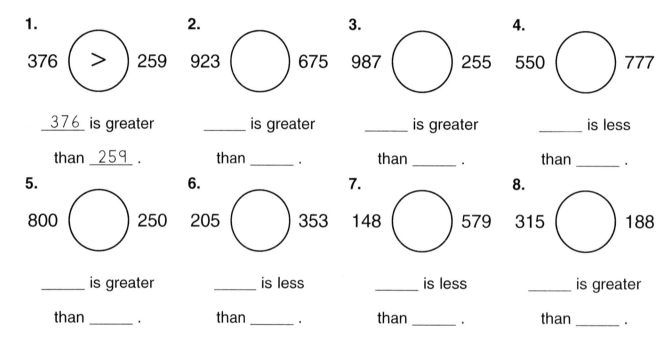

1st   2nd   3rd   4th   5th   6th   7th   8th   9th   10th

9. The square is _____ in line.

10. The oval is _____ in line.

11. The pentagon is _____ in line.

12. The diamond is _____ in line.

13. The cube is _____ in line.

14. The star is _____ in line.

Learning Notes

Children work with place value to 5 places (ten thousands, thousands, hundreds, tens, and ones). They also learn to read 3-, 4-, and 5-digit numbers correctly and identify the name and value of a number based upon its place.

Materials

- 2–3 copies of the place-value block patterns on page 14 for each child
- scissors
- place-value mat (can be made on a piece of paper, as shown in the example on the right)

Ten Thousands	Thousands	Hundreds	Tens	Ones

- envelopes or plastic bags for sorting the place-value models
- 4 six-sided or nine-sided dice for each child
- 4 small paper cups labeled thousands, hundreds, tens, and ones for each child
- 50 index cards numbered 0–9 (5 copies of each number) for each child

Teaching the Lesson

Using Place-Value Blocks (page 14): Enlarge and reproduce (on heavy paper) several copies of the place-value block patterns for children. Have them cut out the patterns and use them as manipulatives on a place-value mat. (An alternative to using a mat is to make labels for each of the place values and place them in the correct order for children to use with the manipulatives.)

Model how to represent several numbers on the place-value mat. For example, to show the number 1,382, ask children what number represents the ones place, the tens place, etc. Show children how to place the correct number of block patterns in the appropriate columns.

After having the opportunity to make different numbers, the children can store the place value blocks in small plastic bags or envelopes.

Using Place Value (page 15): Demonstrate how to shake each cup and record the numbers in the correct place on the practice page and record the place of the pre-selected number.

Making Numbers (page 16): Demonstrate how to lay out the cards in order. Model how to decide whether the number is odd or even, what number comes before the number, and what number comes after the number. (**Note:** Some numbers will require a change in both the ones place and tens place. For example, one more than 36,9**19** is 36,9**20** and one less than 36,9**40** is 36,9**39**.)

Place-Value Block Patterns

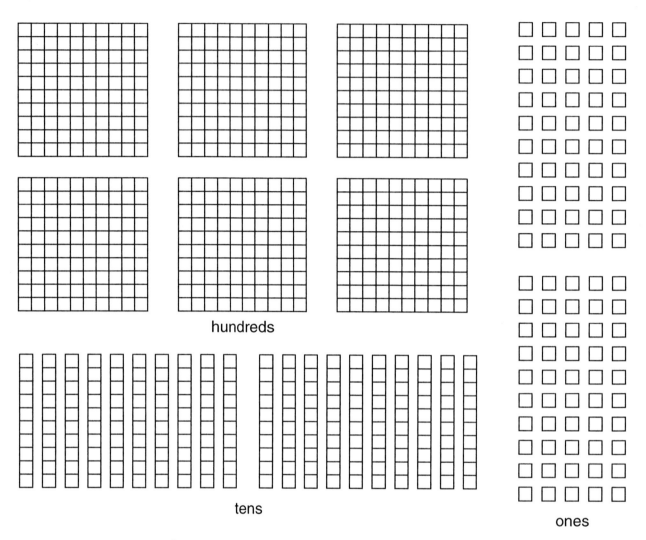

hundreds

tens

ones

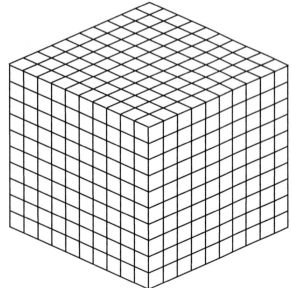

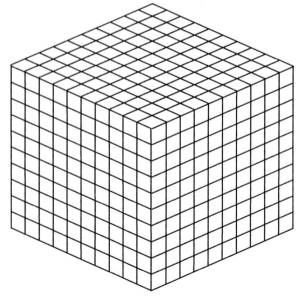

thousands

Label four cups as shown. Place a six-sided or nine-sided die in each cup.

Shake the cups. Record the numbers shown on the die in each cup on the recording sheet below. In the last column, write the place value of the number marked with a ★.

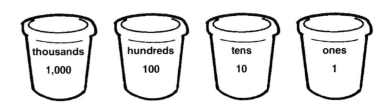

	thousands	hundreds	tens	ones	★ place of selected number
1.	3 ,	8 ★	7	1	hundreds
2.	★ ,				
3.	,			★	
4.	,		★		
5.	,		★		
6.	,	★			
7.	★ ,				
8.	,			★	
9.	★ ,				
10.	★ ,				

11. Write the starred numbers in order from smallest to largest.

_____, _____, _____, _____, _____, _____, _____, _____, _____, _____

12. What was the largest number made? _____

13. What was the smallest number made? _____

14. Write the odd numbers that were made.

_____

15. Write the even numbers that were made.

_____

Take the numbered index cards, shuffle them, and place them in a stack facedown. Turn over the top five cards and lay them out in the order they were turned over. Record the numbers. Write whether the number made is odd or even. (Remember, odd numbers end in 1, 3, 5, 7, or 9 and even numbers end in 0, 2, 4, 6, or 8.) Write the numbers that comes before and after the number made. The first one has been done for you.

number made with the cards	odd or even	number that comes before	number that comes after
1. 3 6 , 9 0 8	even	36,907	36,909
2.			
3.			
4.			
5.			
6.			
7.			
8.			
9.			
10.			

16

Learning Notes

In this unit children learn to round numbers to the nearest tens, hundreds, and thousands. They also use the concept of rounding in addition and subtraction problems.

Materials

- 50 index cards numbered 0–9 (5 sets of each number)
- number line 10–20
- place-value mat (may be made on a piece of paper, as shown in the example on the right)

thousands	hundreds	tens	ones

Teaching the Lesson

Use the number line to introduce the idea of rounding. Color the numbers 10–14 red and the numbers 15–20 blue.

Ask the children if the number 16 is closer to 10 or 20. (*The number is in the blue area so it is closer to 20.*) Do this with several different numbers to give the children visual practice with rounding.

Review the concept of place value, using the place-value mats and numbered index cards. Give each child a set of index cards and a place-value mat. Shuffle the cards and place in a stack facedown. Take the top four cards, turn them over in order, and lay them on the place-value mat in the same order.

thousands	hundreds	tens	ones
4	3	7	6

Look at the number in the ones column. Is the 6 closer to 0 tens or 1 ten (*10*)? (*1 ten*)

Look at the 76. Is it closer to 7 tens (*70*) or 8 tens (*80*)? 0 hundreds or 1 hundred (*100*)?

Continue in this manner, discussing the various numbers in each column. The basic process is the same. If the number is 0 to 4, round down to the next number. If the number is 5 to 9, round up to the next number.

Introduce how to round numbers and go over the work sheets with the children.

Rounding numbers to the nearest tens, hundreds, or thousands is useful when adding several numbers together to reach a total. The total will be an estimate of the actual total.

> Round each number to the nearest tens. If the number in the ones place is 0, 1, 2, 3, or 4, round down to the nearest tens. If the number in the ones place is 5, 6, 7, 8, or 9, round up to the nearest tens.
>
> **Example:** 29 ➤ The number in the ones place is a 9, so round up to 30.
>
> **Example:** 22 ➤ The number in the ones place is a 2, so round down to 20.

Round each number to the nearest 10.

1. 37 _____   **3.** 41 _____   **5.** 73 _____

2. 25 _____   **4.** 62 _____   **6.** 91 _____

> Round each number to the nearest hundreds. If the number in the tens place is 0, 1, 2, 3, or 4, round down to the nearest hundreds. If the number in the tens place is 5, 6, 7, 8, or 9, round up to the nearest hundreds.
>
> **Example:** 164 ➤ The number in the tens place is a 6, so round up to 200.
>
> **Example:** 131 ➤ The number in the tens place is a 3, so round down to 100.

Round each number to the nearest 100.

7. 321 _____   **9.** 491 _____   **11.** 847 _____

8. 578 _____   **10.** 610 _____   **12.** 902 _____

> Round each number to the nearest thousands. If the number in the hundreds place is 0, 1, 2, 3, or 4, round down to the nearest thousands. If the number in the hundreds place is 5, 6, 7, 8, or 9, round up to the nearest thousands.
>
> **Example:** 1,730 ➤ The number in the hundreds place is 7, so round up to 2,000.
>
> **Example:** 1,198 ➤ The number in the hundreds place is 1, so round down to 1,000.

Round each number to the nearest 1,000.

13. 8,190 _____   **15.** 3,943 _____   **17.** 9,209 _____

14. 7,652 _____   **16.** 5,725 _____   **18.** 1,871 _____

Solve each word problem by rounding each number to the nearest tens and then adding or subtracting. Show your work in the space provided.

1. Jason invited 39 girls and 22 boys to his party. How many children did Jason invite in all? The number 39 is rounded to 40. The number 22 is rounded to 20. (40 + 20 = 60) __60__ children were invited to the party.	$$\begin{array}{r} 40 \\ + 20 \\ \hline 60 \end{array}$$
2. Mariah bought 152 balloons, 127 party hats, and 213 candles for the party. How many party items did Mariah buy in all? Mariah bought _____ party items in all.	
3. Beau sent out 185 invitations. 87 people said "yes." The rest said "no." How many people said "no"? _____ people said "no."	
4. Lucy set out 210 green jellybeans, 315 red jellybeans, and 57 orange jellybeans. How many jellybeans did Lucy set out in all? Lucy set out _____ jellybeans.	
5. Sprinkles were put on 3 cupcakes. The children used 567 sprinkles were in all. The first cupcake had 237 sprinkles. The second cupcake had 197. How many sprinkles did the third cupcake have? The third cup cake had _____ sprinkles.	
6. Darts were played at the party. Ben scored 222 points. Jacob scored 303 points. Elena scored 368 points. How many points were scored in all? _____ points were scored in all.	

Write the answers in order from smallest to greatest.

_____, _____, _____, _____, _____, _____,

Look at the number of items in each box. Decide whether to round to the nearest tens, hundreds, or thousands. Circle the "Th" (thousand); "H" (hundred); or "T" (ten) to show which place the item was rounded to. Write the rounded number in the box. The first one has already been done for you.

1.   **2.**   **3.**   **4.**   **5.**

298   28   1,092   11   817

Th (H) T	Th H T	Th H T	Th H T	Th H T
300				

6.   **7.**   **8.**   **9.**   **10.**

2,374   52   4,026   700   5,963

Th H T	Th H T	Th H T	Th H T	Th H T

Round each number to the nearest 100. Add or subtract. The first one has been done for you.

11.

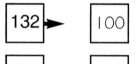

```
132 ▶ 100
406 ▶ + 400
      ─────
        500
```

12.

```
640 ▶ ☐
304 ▶ – ☐
      ─────
        ☐
```

13.

```
515 ▶ ☐
291 ▶ + ☐
      ─────
        ☐
```

14.

```
943 ▶ ☐
757 ▶ – ☐
      ─────
        ☐
```

15.

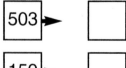

```
503 ▶ ☐
159 ▶ – ☐
      ─────
        ☐
```

16.

```
720 ▶ ☐
617 ▶ – ☐
      ─────
        ☐
```

17.

```
810 ▶ ☐
113 ▶ + ☐
      ─────
        ☐
```

18.

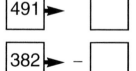

```
491 ▶ ☐
382 ▶ – ☐
      ─────
        ☐
```

Learning Notes

The children will learn to add and subtract 3-, 4-, and 5-digit numbers with one regrouping of numbers.

Materials

- place-value blocks (page 14)
- place-value mat (This can be made on a piece of paper, as shown in the example on the right.)

thousands	hundreds	tens	ones

Teaching the Lesson

Before beginning the pages 22–24 have the children practice addition and subtraction regrouping using place-value mats and blocks.

Addition Example:

$$\begin{array}{r} \overset{1}{17\!4} \\ +\ 40\,8 \\ \hline 58\,2 \end{array}$$

4 + 8 = 12
or
1 ten, 2 ones

Have the children use their place-value blocks to make both numbers. Count the ones (4 + 8 = 12). Take 10 of the ones and exchange for a ten. Record the remaining 2 ones. Move to the tens column and add the numbers (7 + 0 + 1 that was regrouped) and then add the hundreds column.

Subtraction Example:

$$\begin{array}{r} \overset{8\ 11}{4\cancel{9}\cancel{1}} \\ -\ 164 \\ \hline 327 \end{array}$$

1 ten + 1 one = 11
11 − 4 = 7

Because 4 ones can not be subtracted from 1 one, regroup. Take a 10 from the tens column, change the 9 to an 8, and exchange the borrowed ten for 10 ones. Now subtract 4 ones from 11 ones and record the number. Move to the tens column and subtract 6 tens from the remaining 8 tens. Then move to the hundreds column and subtract 1 hundred from 4 hundreds.

Important Note: Reinforce the idea that when adding and subtracting, the children always need to start in the ones column and work from right to left.

When the children have completed a subtraction problem, they can check their answer by adding the difference and the subtrahend together. The answer should be the same as the minuend, the first number that the problem began with.

Example:

$$\begin{array}{r} \overset{1\ 11}{8,6\cancel{2}\cancel{1}} \\ -\ 6,315 \\ \hline 2,306 \end{array} \qquad \begin{array}{r} \overset{1}{\ } \\ 2,306 \\ +\ 6,315 \\ \hline 8,621 \end{array}$$

Go over pages 22–24 with the children.

Start at the ones place. 6 + 6 = 12. That is the same as 1 ten and 2 ones. Write the 2 in the ones place and regroup the 1 ten to the tens place.

```
 [1]
  276
+ 306
------
    2
```

Move to the tens place, add the addends and write the answer. Then continue adding and recording the numbers in the hundreds, thousands, and ten thousands place.

```
 [1]
  276
+ 306
------
  582
```

Solve each addition problem. Remember to regroup when necessary.

1. 844 + 149

2. 237 + 116

3. 403 + 579

4. 106 + 629

5. 6,005 + 2,967

6. 5,789 + 3,203

7. 8,234 + 1,538

8. 8,987 + 1,004

9. 23,809 + 24,173

10. 58,614 + 10,056

11. 65,279 + 23,516

12. 41,747 + 17,248

13. 685 + 9,306

14. 5,802 + 3,069

15. 50,874 + 2,119

16. 8,936 + 11,024

Start at the ones place. 4 cannot be subtracted from 2. Regroup (borrow) a ten from the tens column and add it to the 2 in the ones column. Now subtract 4 from 12 and write the answer.	Move to the tens, hundreds, thousands, and ten thousands columns and subtract the subtrahends from the other numbers. Record each number.	To check your work, add the subtrahend to the difference. The answer should be the same as the number you started with.
$\begin{array}{r} \boxed{0} \\ 6\,\not{7}^{1}\not{2} \\ -\,4\,0\,4 \\ \hline 8 \end{array}$	$\begin{array}{r} \boxed{0} \\ 6\,\not{7}^{1}\not{2} \\ -\,4\,0\,4 \\ \hline 2\,0\,8 \end{array}$	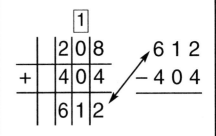

Solve each subtraction problem. Then check your work by using addition. The first one has been done for you.

1. $\begin{array}{r} \boxed{6} \\ \not{8}\,\overset{1}{7}\,3 \\ -\,3\,5\,5 \\ \hline 5\,1\,8 \end{array}$ $\begin{array}{r} \boxed{1} \\ +\quad \begin{array}{|c|c|c|} \hline 5&1&8 \\ \hline 3&5&5 \\ \hline 8&7&3 \\ \hline \end{array} \end{array}$

2. $\begin{array}{r} \square \\ 9\,7\,1 \\ -\,5\,0\,3 \\ \hline \end{array}$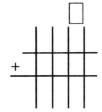

3. $\begin{array}{r} \square \\ 4\,7\,5 \\ -\,1\,3\,6 \\ \hline \end{array}$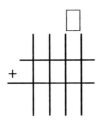

4. $\begin{array}{r} \square \\ 7{,}8\,9\,7 \\ -\,3{,}3\,3\,8 \\ \hline \end{array}$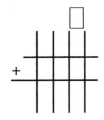

5. $\begin{array}{r} \square \\ 5{,}6\,6\,0 \\ -\,4{,}0\,0\,1 \\ \hline \end{array}$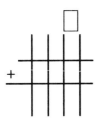

6. $\begin{array}{r} \square \\ 7{,}9\,7\,4 \\ -\,1{,}8\,5\,9 \\ \hline \end{array}$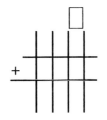

Solve each math problem. Write the letter that goes with the answer on the line at the bottom of the page to discover the secret message.

A	= 10,727	N	= 76,670	S	= 2,343
E	= 7,951	O	= 6,840	U	= 2,117
G	= 777	P	= 31,016	Y	= 963
I	= 45,785	R	= 72,718		

1. 78,745
  – 6,027

2. 6,902
  + 1,049

3. 458
  + 319

4. 98,830
  – 26,112

5. 6,632
  + 208

6. 2,535
  – 418

7. 73,124
  – 42,108

8. 45,479
  + 306

9. 76,037
  + 633

10. 9,892
  – 9,115

11. 83,992
  – 38,207

12. 1,925
  + 418

13. 18,960
  – 11,009

14. 10,945
  – 218

15. 12,950
  – 10,607

16. 535
  + 428

Secret Message:

___ ___ ___ ___ ___ ___ ___ ___ ___ ___
  1   2   3   4   5   6   7   8   9   10

___ ___   ___ ___ ___ ___!
 11 12   13 14 15 16

Learning Notes

In this unit children will learn to regroup twice working with 3-, 4-, and 5-digit addition and subtraction problems. Children will use skills to compare 3-, 4-, and 5-digit numbers. They will also practice skip counting by 2's, 5's, 10's, and 20's.

thousands	hundreds	tens	ones

Materials

- place-value mat (can be made on a piece of paper, as shown in the example on the right)
- place-value blocks
- 50 index cards numbered 0–9 (5 cards of each number)

Teaching the Lesson

Before using pages 26–28 have the children practice regrouping twice using the place value blocks and mats. Do this several times with the children so that they are familiar with the process.

Example: 221 ⟶ 2 hundreds, 1 ten, 11 ones ⟶ 1 hundred, 11 tens, 11 ones

Regrouping Twice when Adding

$$
\begin{array}{r}
1 \\
4{,}668 \\
+\ 3{,}245 \\
\hline
3
\end{array}
$$

8 ones + 5 ones = 13 ones or 1 ten 3 ones ⟶

$$
\begin{array}{r}
11 \\
4{,}668 \\
+\ 3{,}245 \\
\hline
13
\end{array}
$$

1 ten + 6 tens + 4 tens = 11 tens or 1 hundred + 1 ten ⟶

$$
\begin{array}{r}
11 \\
4{,}668 \\
+\ 3{,}245 \\
\hline
7{,}913
\end{array}
$$

Regrouping Twice when Subtracting

$$
\begin{array}{r}
5{,}754 \\
-\ 3{,}277 \\
\hline
\end{array}
$$

7 ones can't be subtracted from 4, so regroup ⟶

$$
\begin{array}{r}
4 \\
5{,}7\cancel{5}4 \\
-\ 3{,}277 \\
\hline
7
\end{array}
$$

7 tens can't be subtracted from 4 tens, so regroup ⟶

$$
\begin{array}{r}
6\ ^1 4 \\
5{,}\cancel{7}\cancel{5}4^{\,1} \\
-\ 3{,}277 \\
\hline
2{,}477
\end{array}
$$

Practice comparing numbers using place-value blocks.

Example: 310   **Example:** 327

Start with the hundreds column. Since both numbers have 3 hundreds, move to the tens column. The number 310 has 1 ten while 327 has 2 tens. Notice that 2 tens are larger than 1 ten. Therefore 327 is larger than 310.

Verbally practice skip counting by 2's, 5's, 10's, and 20's using familiar numbers: 20, 22, 24, 26, etc. Then move to unfamiliar numbers: 137, 139, 141, 143, etc.

Go over pages 26–28 with the children.

Start on the ones place. Notice that 9 ones + 1 one equals 10 and 10 is 1 ten and 0 ones. Write the zero in the ones column and regroup the 1 ten to the tens column.	Move to the tens column. There are 7 tens + 5 tens + the 1 ten that was regrouped. 7 + 5 + 1 = 13 tens or 1 hundred and 3 tens. Write the 3 in the tens column and carry the 1 to the hundreds column.	Finally, move to the hundreds column. 6 hundreds + 1 hundred + 1 hundred (that was regrouped) = 8 hundreds. Write the 8 in the hundreds column.

$\boxed{1}$
 679
 + 1 5 1
 ———
     0
	$\boxed{1}\boxed{1}$
	 679
	 + 1 5 1
	 ———
	   3 0
		$\boxed{1}\boxed{1}$
		 679
		 + 1 5 1
		 ———
		 8 3 0

Solve each addition problem.

1.   □□
 563
 + 258

2.   □□
 188
 + 549

3.   □□
 479
 + 259

4.   □□
 689
 + 113

5.   □□
 2,723
 + 6,097

6.   □□
 1,067
 + 3,063

7.   □□
 5,487
 + 1,238

8.   □□
 8,049
 + 1,454

9.   □□
 53,186
 + 20,018

Look at each pair of numbers. Circle the larger one. Which place did you look at when deciding which number was the largest?

10. (185)   102   _tens_   **13.** 2,713   3,713   _____

11. 3,589   3,579   _____   **14.** 679   605   _____

12. 427   879   _____   **15.** 4,901   5,003   _____

Start on the ones place. Notice that 8 ones can not be subtracted from 1 one. Regroup (borrow) a ten from the tens column and add it to the 1 one. Subtract 8 from 11.	Move to the tens column. Notice that 9 tens can not be subtracted from 0 tens. Regroup a hundred from the hundreds column. Subtract 9 tens from 10 tens.	Finally, move to the hundreds column (thousands and ten thousands columns as needed) and finish subtracting each number. Record the answers.
⬚0̸ 11 4 X̸ X̸ − 1 9 8 ──── 3	10 3 0̸ 11 A̸ X̸ X̸ − 1 9 8 ──── 1 3	10 3 0̸ 11 A̸ X̸ X̸ − 1 9 8 ──── 2 1 3

Solve each subtraction problem.

1. 751
   − 382

2. 964
   − 376

3. 983
   − 894

4. 635
   − 577

5. 3,828
   − 1,049

6. 7,240
   − 4,166

7. 5,241
   − 3,067

8. 7,532
   − 2,168

9. 19,338
   − 15,279

Look at each set of numbers. Write the missing numbers.

10. 631, 641, _____ , _____ , _____ , 681

11. 1,086, 1,091, _____ , _____ , 1,106, _____ ,1,116

12. 1,472, 1,475, _____ , 1,481, _____ , _____ , 1,490

13. 4,084, 4,074, _____ , _____ , _____

14. 79,320, 79,420, _____ , _____ , _____

Shuffle the numbered index cards and place them in a stack facedown. Take the top 5 cards and turn them over. Record the numbers in the same order as they were turned over. Take the next 5 cards and record the numbers below the first set of numbers. Decide whether the second number can be subtracted from the first or if the numbers have to be added. Write either + or − in the circle and solve the problem. The first one has been done for you.

1.
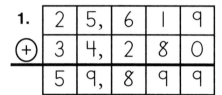

2	5,	6	1	9
3	4,	2	8	0
5	9,	8	9	9

(+)

2.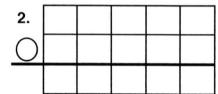

3.

4.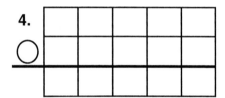

5.

6.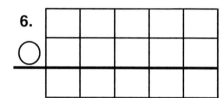

7.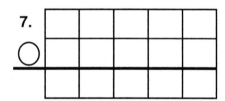

8.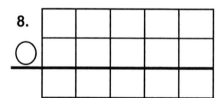

9.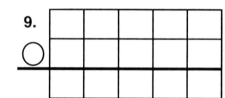

10.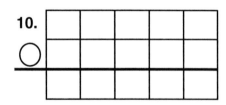

11.

12.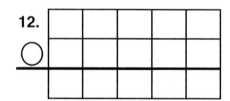

Write the missing numbers.

13. 216, 218, 220, _____ , _____ , _____ , 228, _____ , 232

14. 445, 450, _____ , _____ , 465, _____ , _____ , _____ , 485

15. 321, 331, _____ , 351, _____ , _____ , _____ , 391, _____

16. 564, 584, _____ , 624, _____ , _____ , _____ , _____ , 724

Learning Notes

Children learn to write numbers in expanded form using words only, numbers only, and numbers and words.

Materials

- 3 dice for each child

- poster of the following math vocabulary chart

Expanded Form			Standard Form
Words Only	**Numbers & Words**	**Numbers Only**	**Standard**
two hundred fifty three thousand, four hundred twelve	2 hundred thousands 5 ten thousands 3 thousands 4 hundreds 1 ten 2 ones	200,000 50,000 3,000 400 10 2 (or) 200,000 + 50,000+ 3,000 + 400 + 10+ 2	253,412

Teaching the Lesson

Before beginning the work sheets, ask the children for another way to write the number 27. Show the children that 27 is the same as 2 tens 7 ones *or* 20 + 7 (or 27)

Have the children practice writing different 2-, 3-, 4-, and 5-digit numbers using the expanded form. Go over the work sheets with the children. Remind the children to refer to the chart for help if needed.

Learning Tip

Make a photocopy of the chart for each student to keep as a reference tool.

Numbers can be written in standard form or expanded form.

Standard Form		**Expanded Form**
295	**or**	200 + 90 + 5
		(hundreds) (tens) (ones)

Roll three dice. Record the number that appears on top in both standard form and expanded form.

Numbers Rolled	**Standard Form**	**Expanded Form**
⚂ ⚃ ⚀	341	300 + 40 + 1
1. ⬜ ⬜ ⬜		
2. ⬜ ⬜ ⬜		
3. ⬜ ⬜ ⬜		
4. ⬜ ⬜ ⬜		
5. ⬜ ⬜ ⬜		
6. ⬜ ⬜ ⬜		
7. ⬜ ⬜ ⬜		

What was the smallest number made?_____

What was the largest number made? _____

Read the number in the written form. Then write the number in the expanded form and also in standard form.

Written Form	Expanded Form	Standard Form
1. three hundred forty-two thousand, two hundred ten	300,000 + 40,000 + 2,000 + 200 + 10	342,210
2. three hundred forty-five thousand, sixteen		
3. five hundred thirty thousand, two hundred one		
4. seven hundred fifty thousand, nine hundred eleven		
5. four hundred seventy-six thousand, eight hundred twenty		
6. one hundred thousand, four hundred thirty-seven		
7. eight hundred sixty-one thousand, one hundred ninety-two		

Numbers can also be written in expanded form using words.

Examples:

589 is the same as 5 hundreds + 8 tens + 9 ones

85,901 is the same as 8 ten thousands + 5 thousands + 9 hundreds + 1 one

Write the following numbers in expanded form using words.

1. 623 _____

_____

2. 5,012 _____

_____

3. 30,968 _____

_____

4. 208 _____

_____

5. 73,997 _____

_____

6. 8,647 _____

_____

7. 356,911 _____

_____

8. 415,827 _____

_____

9. 442 _____

_____

10. 6,928 _____

_____

Write the numbers in order from smallest to greatest.

_____ , _____ , _____ , _____ , _____ ,

_____ , _____ , _____ , _____ , _____

Learning Notes

Children recognize decimals to two places (tenths and hundredths). They add and subtract numbers with decimal points and learn to write numbers with decimals using words and numbers.

Materials

- lined notebook paper

Teaching the Lesson

Explain to the children that decimals are used every day in fractions, in money, as percentages on test scores, etc.

Go over the vocabulary of decimals: tenths and hundredths. Tenths are $\frac{1}{10}$ of the whole. A dime is one-tenth of a dollar. It takes 10 dimes to make $1.00.

Hundredths are $\frac{1}{100}$ of the whole. A penny is one-hundredth of a dollar. It takes 100 pennies to make $1.00.

Using lined paper, show the children how to turn the paper sideways and then write the numbers with decimal points. The lines make columns. This makes it easier for the children to line up the numbers and the decimal points.

Go over pages 34–36 with the children. Demonstrate that adding and subtracting numbers with decimal points is done the same way as numbers without decimal points.

Learning Tip

Remind the children of the importance of writing the decimal point in the answers. For example, explain that without the decimal 2,650 is not the same as 26.50. 2,650 is two thousand, six hundred fifty. The number 26.50 is twenty-six and five-tenths. (The "and" takes the place of the decimal point when the number is read aloud.)

```
        3 9 . 6 1
      + 2 0 . 3 7
        5 9 . 9 8
```

Decimals are used in writing fractions and in showing different amounts of money.

Example:

$\frac{2}{10}$ is the same as .2; both are read as two tenths.

25¢ is the same as $0.25; both are read as twenty-five cents.

The numbers to the left of the decimal point show whole numbers.

The numbers to the right of the decimal point show a fraction of a number.

tens	ones	decimal point	tenths	hundredths
1	**4**	**.**	**3**	**5**

This number has
1 ten (10.0)
4 ones (4.0)
3 tenths (.3)
5 hundredths (.05)

Look at each number. Circle the correct way to read the number. The first one has already been done for you.

1. .8   eight hundredths

(eight tenths)

2. .01   one hundredth

one tenth

3. .9   nine tenths

nine hundredths

4. .06   six tenths

six hundredths

5. .75   seventy-five hundredths

seventy-five tenths

6. .42   forty-two tenths

forty-two hundredths

Write the number word using numerals.

7. 3 tenths _____

8. 29 hundredths _____

9. 7 hundredths _____

10. 81 hundredths _____

11. 4 tenths _____

12. 5 hundredths _____

13. 6 hundredths _____

14. 1 tenth _____

When adding and subtracting numbers with decimals, make sure you line up the decimal point in each number. Then add or subtract beginning in the hundredths column and moving to the next column on the left.

$$\begin{array}{r} 85.14 \\ +\ 11.65 \\ \hline 96.79 \end{array} \qquad \begin{array}{r} 93.82 \\ -\ 22.11 \\ \hline 71.71 \end{array}$$

Solve each math problem.

1. $\begin{array}{r} 93.82 \\ -\ 60.31 \\ \hline \end{array}$
2. $\begin{array}{r} 14.86 \\ +\ 84.02 \\ \hline \end{array}$
3. $\begin{array}{r} 24.37 \\ +\ 54.32 \\ \hline \end{array}$
4. $\begin{array}{r} 93.74 \\ -\ 92.62 \\ \hline \end{array}$

5. $\begin{array}{r} 37.58 \\ +\ 52.30 \\ \hline \end{array}$
6. $\begin{array}{r} 68.46 \\ -\ 17.02 \\ \hline \end{array}$
7. $\begin{array}{r} 57.32 \\ -\ 34.00 \\ \hline \end{array}$
8. $\begin{array}{r} 85.32 \\ +\ 10.46 \\ \hline \end{array}$

9. $\begin{array}{r} 97.98 \\ -\ 10.10 \\ \hline \end{array}$
10. $\begin{array}{r} 66.95 \\ -\ 26.10 \\ \hline \end{array}$
11. $\begin{array}{r} 87.32 \\ +\ 11.50 \\ \hline \end{array}$
12. $\begin{array}{r} 28.81 \\ +\ 41.08 \\ \hline \end{array}$

Read and solve each word problem. Show your work.

13. Jessica went shopping. She spent $14.10 buying a shirt and $23.67 buying a pair of shoes. How much money did Jessica spend in all?

$$+\ \underline{\qquad \cdot \qquad}$$

14. Tyrone had $38.59 in his piggy bank. He spent $25.06 buying a video game. How much money does Tyrone have left?

$$-\ \underline{\qquad \cdot \qquad}$$

When adding numbers with decimals, always start in the hundredths column (6 + 6 = 12). This is the same as 2 hundredths and 1 tenth. Write the 2 in the hundredths column and regroup the 1 to the tenths column. Add the 1 tenth to the 4 + 9. That makes 14 or 1 one and 4 tenths. Write the 4 in the tenths column and the 1 in the ones column. Then add the numbers in the ones column and the tens column.	1 1 47.46 + 41.96 89.42	When subtracting, always start in the hundredths column. Since 8 cannot be subtracted from 7, regroup by changing the 5 in the tenths column to a 4. Now, there are 17 hundredths − 8 hundredths. Write the answer. Move to the tenths column. Since 9 can not be subtracted from 4, regroup by changing the 7 to a 6. There are 14 tenths − 9 tenths. Write the answer. Then subtract the numbers in the ones column and the tens column. Write the answers.	6 4 17 57.57 − 11.98 45.59

Solve each problem below.

1. 38.14
    + 10.99

2. 12.66
    + 22.88

3. 55.44
    − 32.96

4. 53.60
    − 11.72

5. 93.30
    − 34.99

6. 40.57
    + 53.97

7. 82.45
    − 80.67

8. 36.77
    + 52.84

9. 10.05
    + 34.99

10. 95.13
    − 62.76

11. 10.79
    + 76.98

12. 48.40
    − 32.49

Add .1 (1 tenth) to each number.

13. 34.78 _____

14. 78.50 _____

15. 95.71 _____

16. 12.61 _____

Subtract .1 (1 tenth) from each number.

17. 20.14 _____

18. 36.95 _____

19. 36.29 _____

20. 64.72 _____

36

9 How to ••••••••••••• Use Graphs and Charts with Decimals

Learning Notes

Children make a graph from given information and answer questions based upon the information. They add and subtract 3-, 4-, and 5-digit numbers with and without regrouping. Children also add and subtract 3-, 4-, and 5-digit numbers with decimal points.

Materials

- lined notebook paper
- calculators

Teaching the Lesson

Pages 38–40 present a three-part investigation. The pages must be completed in order because the information from one page is needed to complete the next page.

Using Chart Information (page 38): Demonstrate how to create a two-color graph using the information in the chart.

Applying Data to Solve Problems (page 39) and Solving Problems Using Charts (page 40): The children need to find differences between each place's daily pass rate and weekend pass rate. The children will then use this information to answer the questions at the bottom of each page. (Have calculators available for the children to use to check the accuracy of their work.)

Learning Tip

Remind the children to turn the lined paper sideways and then write the addition or subtraction problem. Make sure the decimal points and numbers are lined up in each column before solving the math problem.

	○					○					○
					2	1	.	1	4		
				+	1	6	.	3	4		
					3	7	.	4	8		

Place	Daily Pass Rate	Weekend Pass Rate
Waterslide	$67.31	$71.65
Amusement Park	$175.88	$289.24
Safari Adventureland	$82.44	$151.78
Movie Studio	$32.99	$57.90
Wax Museum	$149.26	$281.37
Cartoon Land	$221.70	$336.52

Make a graph showing each place's daily rate and weekend pass rate. Use a green crayon to show the daily pass rate and a red crayon to show the weekend pass rate.

	Daily Rate	Week-end	Daily Rate	Week-end	Daily Rate	Week-end	Daily Rate	Week-end	Daily Rate	Week-end	Daily Rate	Week-end
$301–$350												
$251–$300												
$201–$250												
$151–$200												
$101–$150												
$51–$100												
$0–$50												
	Waterslide		Amusement Park		Safari Adventureland		Movie Studio		Wax Museum		Cartoon Land	

Place	Daily Pass Rate	Weekend Pass Rate
Waterslide	$67.31	$71.65
Amusement Park	$175.88	$289.24
Safari Adventureland	$82.44	$151.78
Movie Studio	$32.99	$57.90
Wax Museum	$149.26	$281.37
Cartoon Land	$221.70	$336.52

Use the information above to find the difference between each place's daily pass rate and weekend pass rate.

1. Waterslide	**2.** Amusement Park	**3.** Safari Adventureland
4. Movie Studio	**5.** Wax Museum	**6.** Cartoon Land

7. Which place had the greatest difference between its daily pass rate and its weekend pass rate? _____

8. Which place had the smallest difference between its daily pass rate and weekend pass rate? _____

9. How much would it cost to visit both the Waterslide and Cartoon Land for a weekday?

   _____

10. How much would it cost to visit both the Movie Studio and the Amusement Park for a weekday? _____

11. If you had $250 to spend, what would be the greatest number of places you could visit in a day? List the places and the total cost. _____

    _____

12. If you had $250 to spend, what would be the fewest number of places you could visit? List the place(s) and the total cost for a day. _____

    _____

Good news! Each place is offering a special discount on their daily passes and weekend passes.

- Each daily pass is $8.25 less.

- Each weekend pass is $16.50 less.

Use the chart below to write the new prices for each daily pass rate and weekend pass rate. (Show your work on a separate piece of paper.)

Place	Old Daily Pass Rate	New Daily Pass Rate	Old Weekend Pass Rate	New Weekend Pass Rate
Waterslide	$67.31	1. _____	$71.65	2. _____
Amusement Park	$175.88	3. _____	$289.24	4. _____
Safari Adventureland	$82.44	5. _____	$151.78	6. _____
Movie Studio	$32.99	7. _____	$57.90	8. _____
Wax Museum	$149.26	9. _____	$281.37	10. _____
Cartoon Land	$221.70	11. _____	$336.52	12. _____

13. How much money would you save if you visited all of the places at the new daily rate instead of the old daily rate? _____

14. How much would you save if you bought weekend passes to all of the places at the new rate instead of the old rate? _____

15. How many places could you visit in a day at the new daily rate if you had $250? List the places and the total cost. _____

_____

_____

16. Were you able to visit more places with the new daily rates or the old daily rates?

_____

_____

_____

Read each clue. Put an "X" on the number(s) that do not fit each clue. After answering all of the clues, there will be one number left.

805,457	879	80,121	579
2,157	39,643	29,253	144,384
66,175	9,780	7,418	102

Clues

1. When my digits are added together, the total is a number between 20 through 30.

2. There is one 7 in my number.

3. There are more than 3 digits in my number.

4. If you add and subtract each number in order, the answer is less than 10. (**Example:** 579, 5 + 7 − 9 = 3)

5. I have more even digits than odd digits.

6. Which number am I? _____

7. Write a clue that would fit the mystery number. _____

_____

_____

_____

Use the numbers 340, 341, 342, 343, 344, 345, 346, 347, 348, 349, 350, 351, 352, 353, 354, and 355 to make each row and column add up to 1,390. Each number can be used only one time. Write the correct number in each box. (*Hint:* Write each number on a small sticky note. Then move the notes around until the puzzle is solved.)

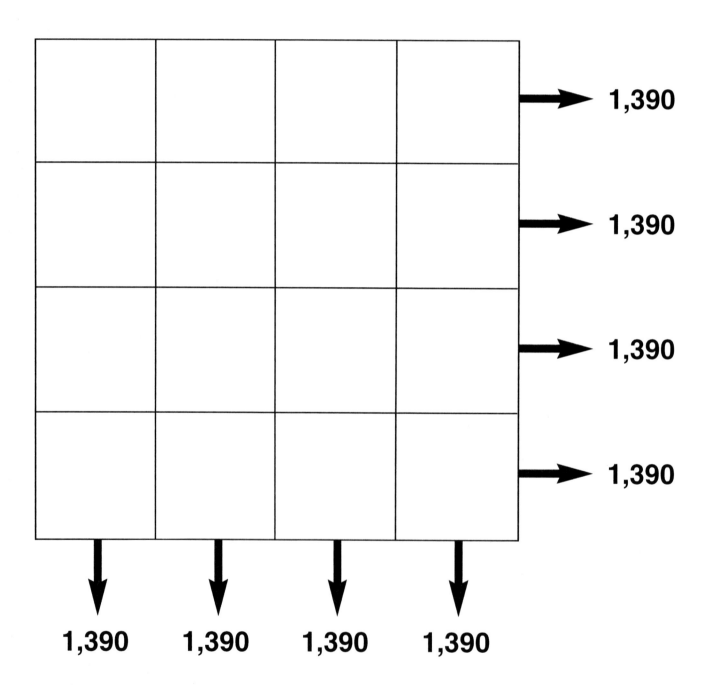

Color one-half of each shape. Write the fraction for each shape.

10. 11. 12. 13.

14. What do you notice about the fractions? _____

Color one-third of each shape. Write the fraction for each shape.

15. 16. 17. 18.

19. What do you notice about the fractions? _____

A fraction is a part of a whole item
Fractions are written like this: $\dfrac{2\ \textbf{(numerator)}}{5\ \textbf{(denominator)}}$

The top number is the **numerator**. The numerator tells us how many parts are used or are needed.
The bottom number is the **denominator**. The denominator tells how many parts there are in all.

Look at each shape. Circle the fraction that tells how many part(s) of each object are shaded.

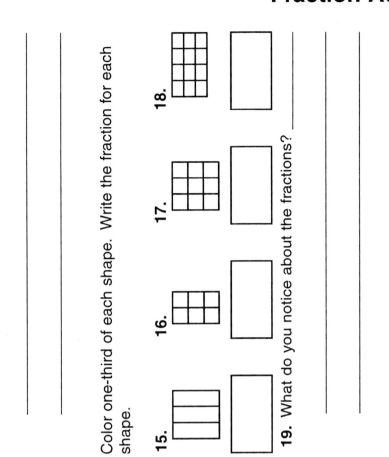

1.

2	3	3
3	5	6

2.

1	1	3
3	4	4

3.

1	2	3
4	4	4

4.

2	2	3
3	5	5

5.

3	3	5
5	8	8

Look at the fractions below. Answer the questions on a separate piece of paper.

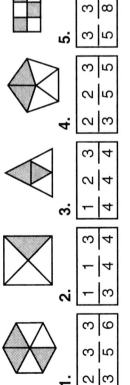

$\dfrac{1}{2}$ $\dfrac{1}{3}$ $\dfrac{1}{4}$ $\dfrac{1}{5}$ $\dfrac{1}{6}$

6. What happens to each piece of pie as the denominator becomes larger?

7. Why does this happen?

8. Which fraction would make the biggest piece of pie?

9. Which fraction would make the smallest piece of pie?

Fractions can be written as decimals.

Example:

$\frac{1}{2}$ = .50 $\frac{1}{3}$ = .33 $\frac{1}{4}$ = .25

Write each fraction as a decimal. Use the chart to help you. Then choose three shapes below and write a fraction or decimal word problem for each. Use the back of this paper.

.25	.33	.40	.50	.60	.67	.75	.80
$\frac{1}{4}$	$\frac{1}{3}$	$\frac{2}{5}$	$\frac{1}{2}$	$\frac{3}{5}$	$\frac{2}{3}$	$\frac{3}{4}$	$\frac{4}{5}$
$\frac{2}{8}$	$\frac{2}{6}$		$\frac{2}{4}$		$\frac{6}{9}$	$\frac{6}{8}$	
	$\frac{3}{9}$		$\frac{3}{6}$				

1.
$\frac{2}{6}$ = _____

2.
$\frac{6}{8}$ = _____

3.
$\frac{2}{3}$ = _____

4.
$\frac{1}{2}$ = _____

5.
$\frac{2}{6}$ = _____

6.
$\frac{2}{8}$ = _____

7.
$\frac{1}{2}$ = _____

8.
$\frac{4}{5}$ = _____

9.
$\frac{2}{4}$ = _____

10.
$\frac{1}{4}$ = _____

11.
$\frac{3}{4}$ = _____

12.
$\frac{6}{9}$ = _____

13.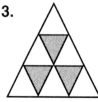
$\frac{3}{9}$ = _____

14.
$\frac{3}{5}$ = _____

15.
$\frac{1}{4}$ = _____

In this activity students will combine coins to come up with as many possible ways to make $1.00 as they can find.

Materials

- samples of U. S. coins
- color code and combinations charts (page 46)
- any drawing programs such as *Kid Pix®*, *HyperStudio®*, etc.

Internet Links

http://pages.prodigy.com/kidsmoney/kids.htm

http://www.usmint.gov/

Teacher Note: Start this activity by providing students either in groups or individually, with samples of all current U. S. coins. Attempt to get all students to differentiate between a half-dollar, quarter, dime, nickel, and penny. Also discuss the relative values that these coins have (one nickel equals five pennies, one dime equals two nickels).

Directions

1. You will create 2 half dollars, 4 quarters, 10 dimes, 10 nickels, and 10 pennies. Keep the proportions between the coins the same (i.e., a dime is not bigger than a nickel). Using the Copy and Paste functions found in nearly all drawing programs will make this an easy task.

2. You may want to make each coin a different color and create a color code to differentiate between coins.

3. Once all of the coins have been created, the task is to combine them in as many ways as possible so that the sum equals $1.00. You must move the coins around on the screen to come up with a combination that totals $1.00. Record this combination on the sheet that is found on the next page and then look for other combinations. After all possible combinations have been found, be sure to save your work. What combination requires the greatest number of coins to make a sum equal to $1.00?

Extension

Move several different coins to the center of the screen and ask a classmate or friend to guess what the value is of these coins. Similarly, have a classmate or friend move several different coins to the center of the screen and find out what all of the coins add up to!

1. What was the most difficult part of this activity?

2. Is there another way to do this activity?

3. Make up a game to play with a partner using what was created on the computer screen.

Color Code Chart: Use this chart to make a color code of the coins.

COIN	Half-Dollar	Quarter	Dime	Nickel	Penny
COLOR					

Fill in this chart with combinations that equal $1.00

Attempts	Half-Dollar	Quarter	Dime	Nickel	Penny	Total $
#1	2					$1.00

Page 6

1.	18	16.	0	31.	6
2.	10	17.	12	32.	5
3.	16	18.	4	33.	−
4.	11	19.	17	34.	+
5.	14	20.	9	35.	+
6.	3	21.	11	36.	−
7.	7	22.	8	37.	+
8.	9	23.	16	38.	−
9.	15	24.	15	39.	+
10.	12	25.	14	40.	+ or −
11.	11	26.	0	41.	+
12.	0	27.	10	42.	−
13.	0	28.	0	43.	+
14.	8	29.	0	44.	+
15.	0	30.	17		

Page 7

1.	18	11.	15
2.	18	12.	15
3.	17	13.	18
4.	17	14.	18
5.	18	15.	14
6.	18	16.	14
7.	14	17.	7 + 5 = 12
8.	14	18.	5 + 7 = 12
9.	14	19.	Sentences will vary.
10.	14	20.	5 + 8 = 13, 8 + 5 = 13

Page 8

1. 3 + 7 = 10; 7 + 3 = 10; 10 − 7 = 3; 10 − 3 = 7
2. 4 + 9 = 13; 9 + 4 = 13; 13 − 9 = 4; 13 − 4 = 9
3. 2 + 15 = 17; 15 + 2 = 17; 17 − 2 = 15; 17 − 15 = 2
4. 6 + 11 = 17; 11 + 6 = 17; 17 − 6 = 11; 17 − 11 = 6
5. 1 + 16 = 17; 16 + 1 = 17; 17 − 1 = 16; 17 − 16 = 1
6. 5 + 13 = 18; 13 + 5 = 18; 18 − 5 = 13; 18 − 13 = 5
7. +, −
8. −, +
9. +, + or −
10. +, −
11. −, +
12. +, −
13. 16 − 6 = 10 − 3 = 7 horses
14. 6 − 3 = 3 more sheep
15. 7 − 3 = 4 more horses
16. 7 − 6 = 1 fewer sheep
17. sheep + horses (6 + 7 = 13)
18. horses − sheep (7 − 6 = 1)

Page 10

1. addends 123, 300; sum 423
2. addends 160, 125; sum 285
3. addends 407, 312; sum 719
4. addends 525, 330; sum 855
5. addends 222, 333; sum 555
6. addends 709, 270; sum 979
7. 227, 352
8. 579
9. 419, 560
10. 979
11. 255 + 400 = 655
12. 158 + 511 = 669

Page 11

1. 321
2. 311
3. 600
4. 241
5. 311
6. 321
7. 749
8. 210
9. 539
10. 428
11. 310
12. 118
13. 567 − 246 = 321
14. 821 − 301 = 520

Page 12

1. 376 > 259; 376 is greater than 259.
2. 923 > 675; 923 is greater than 675.
3. 987 > 255; 987 is greater than 255.
4. 550 < 777; 550 is less than 777.
5. 800 > 250; 800 is greater than 250.
6. 205 < 353; 205 is less than 353.
7. 148 < 579; 148 is less than 579.
8. 315 > 188; 315 is greater than 188.
9. 1st
10. 5th
11. 10th
12. 6th
13. 9th
14. 3rd

Pages 15 and 16

Answers will vary.

Page 18

1.	40	7.	300	13.	8,000
2.	30	8.	600	14.	8,000
3.	40	9.	500	15.	4,000
4.	60	10.	600	16.	6,000
5.	70	11.	800	17.	9,000
6.	90	12.	900	18.	2,000

Page 19

1. 40 + 20 = 60; 60 children were invited to the party.
2. 150 + 130 + 210 = 490; Mariah bought 490 items in all.
3. 190 − 90 = 100; 100 people said "no."
4. 210 + 320 + 60 = 590; Lucy set out 590 jellybeans.
5. 570 − 240 = 330 − 200 = 130; The third cupcake had 130 sprinkles.
6. 220 + 300 + 370 = 890; 890 points were scored in all.

60, 100, 130, 490, 590, 890

Page 20

1. H 300
2. T 30
3. Th 1,000 or H 1,100 or T 1,090
4. T 10
5. H 800 or T 820
6. Th 2,000 or H 2,400 or T 2,370
7. T 50
8. Th 4,000 or H 4,000 or T 4,030
9. Th 1,000 or H 700
10. Th 6,000 or H 6,000 or T 5,960
11. 100 + 400 = 500
12. 600 − 300 = 300

13. 500 + 300 = 800
14. 900 − 800 = 100
15. 500 + 200 = 700
16. 700 − 600 = 100
17. 800 + 100 = 900
18. 500 − 400 = 100

Page 22

1.	993	9.	47,982
2.	353	10.	68,670
3.	982	11.	88,795
4.	735	12.	58,995
5.	8,972	13.	9,991
6.	8,992	14.	8,871
7.	9,772	15.	52,993
8.	9,991	16.	19,960

Page 23

1. 518
   518 + 355 = 873
2. 468
   468 + 503 = 971
3. 339
   339 + 136 = 475
4. 4,559
   4,559 + 3,338 = 7,897
5. 1,659
   1,659 + 4,001 = 5,660
6. 6,115
   6,115 + 1,859 = 7,974

Page 24

1.	72,718	10.	777
2.	7,951	11.	45,785
3.	777	12.	2,343
4.	72,718	13.	7,951
5.	6,840	14.	10,727
6.	2,117	15.	2,343
7.	31,016	16.	963
8.	45,785		
9.	76,670		

Message: Regrouping is easy!

Page 26

1.	821		
2.	737	9.	73,204
3.	738	10.	185; tens
4.	802	11.	3,589; tens
5.	8,820	12.	879; hundreds
6.	4,130	13.	3,713; thousands
7.	6,725	14.	679; tens
8.	9,503	15.	5,003; thousands

Page 27

1. 369
2. 588
3. 89
4. 58
5. 2,779
6. 3,074
7. 2,174
8. 5,364
9. 4,059
10. 651, 661, 671
11. 1,096; 1,101; 1,111
12. 1,478; 1,484; 1,487
13. 4,064, 4,054, 4,044
14. 79,520; 79,620; 79,720; 79,820

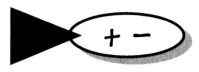

Page 28
1. 59,899
2.–12. Answers will vary.
13. 222, 224, 226, 230
14. 455, 460, 470, 475, 480
15. 341, 361, 371, 381, 401
16. 604, 644, 664, 684, 704

Page 30
Answers will vary.

Page 31
1. 300,000 + 40,000 + 2,000 + 200 + 10; 342,210
2. 300,000 + 40,000 + 5,000 + 10 + 6; 345,016
3. 500,000 + 30,000 + 200 + 1; 530,201
4. 700,000 + 50,000 + 900 + 10 + 1; 750,911
5. 400,000 + 70,000 + 6,000 + 800 + 20; 476,820
6. 100,000 + 400 + 30 + 7; 100,437
7. 800,000 + 60,000 + 1,000 + 100 + 90 + 2; 861,192

Page 32
1. 6 hundreds + 2 tens + 3 ones
2. 5 thousands + 1 ten + 2 ones
3. 3 ten thousands + 9 hundreds + 6 tens + 8 ones
4. 2 hundreds + 8 ones
5. 7 ten thousands + 3 thousands + 9 hundreds + 9 tens + 7 ones
6. 8 thousands + 6 hundreds + 4 tens + 7 ones
7. 3 hundred thousands + 5 ten thousands + 6 thousands + 9 hundreds + 1 ten + 1 one
8. 4 hundred thousands + 1 ten thousand + 5 thousands + 8 hundreds + 2 tens + 7 ones
9. 4 hundreds + 4 tens + 2 ones
10. 6 thousands + 9 hundreds + 2 tens + 8 ones

208; 442; 623; 5,012; 6,928; 8,647; 30,968; 73,997; 356,911; 415,827

Page 34
1. eight tenths
2. one hundredth
3. nine tenths
4. six hundredths
5. seventy-five hundredths
6. forty-two hundredths
7. .3
8. .29
9. .07
10. .81
11. .4
12. .05
13. .06
14. .1

Page 35
1. 33.51
2. 98.88
3. 78.69
4. 1.12
5. 89.88
6. 51.44
7. 23.32
8. 95.78
9. 87.88
10. 40.85
11. 98.82
12. 69.89

13. $14.10 + $23.67 = $37.77
14. $38.59 – $25.06 = $13.53

Page 36
1. 49.13
2. 35.54
3. 22.48
4. 41.88
5. 58.31
6. 94.54
7. 1.78
8. 89.61
9. 45.04
10. 32.37
11. 87.77
12. 15.91
13. 34.88
14. 78.60
15. 95.81
16. 12.71
17. 20.04
18. 36.85
19. 36.19
20. 64.62

Page 38

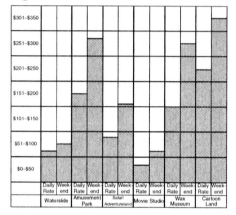

Page 39
1. $71.65 – $67.31 = $4.34
2. $289.24 – $175.88 = $113.36
3. $151.78 – $82.44 = $69.34
4. $57.90 – $32.99 = $24.91
5. $281.37 – $149.26 = $132.11
6. $336.52 – $221.70 = $114.82
7. Wax Museum
8. Waterslide
9. $67.31 + $221.70 = $289.01
10. $32.99 + $175.88 = $208.87
11. Answers will vary.
12. 1 place; Cartoon Land $221.70

Page 40
1. $59.06
2. $55.15
3. $167.63
4. $272.74
5. $74.19
6. $135.28
7. $24.74
8. $41.40
9. $141.01
10. $264.87
11. $213.45
12. $320.02

13. $49.50
14. $99.00
15. Answers will vary.
16. new daily rates.

Page 41
1. cross off 2,157; 80,121; 7,418; 102
2. cross off 39,643; 29,253; 144,384
3. cross off 879; 579
4. cross off 66,175
5. cross off 9,780
6. 805,457
7. Answers will vary.

Page 42
This is just one solution.
1st row: 340; 344; 351; 355
2nd row: 347; 343; 352; 348
3rd row: 349; 350; 345; 346
4th row: 354; 353; 342; 341

Page 43
1. 3/6
2. 1/4
3. 2/4
4. 2/5
5. 3/8
6. The piece of pie becomes smaller.
7. The pie is cut into more pieces.
8. 1/2
9. 1/6
10. 1/2
11. 2/4
12. 3/6
13. 4/8
14. The fractions are the same.
15. 1/3
16. 2/6
17. 3/9
18. 4/12
19. The fractions are the same.

Page 44
1. .33
2. .75
3. .67
4. .50
5. .33
6. .25
7. .50
8. .80
9. .50
10. .25
11. .75
12. .67
13. .33
14. .60
15. .25